CEO-Stories

Children Employed by Owners

Mike Eastwood

Absolute Author
Publishing House

CEO-Stories
Copyright © 2020 by Mike Eastwood
All Rights Reserved

Publisher: Absolute Author Publishing House
Publication Editor: Dr. Melissa Caudle
First Draft Editor: James Millington
Copyline Editor: Shannon Haupe
Cover Designer: Rebeca @RebecaCovers

LIBRARY OF CONGRESS CATALOGUE IN-PUBLICATION-DATA
CEO-Stories/MIKE EASTWOOD

    p. cm.

ISBN: 978-1-64953-035-6

    1. Memoir 2. Non-fiction 3. Business

DEDICATION

I would like to dedicate this book to all the employees who ever worked with me -- the many committed individuals who worked long hours and made each business I managed successfully because of them. With myself gone from the companies, they have been quietly and faithfully going about their business with the knowledge that a company can be amazing with the right leaders in place. After reading this book, I wish you success and never have a company you work for be a CEO-Story.

I like to thank my family for all the years I was gone traveling as they held up the home front, looking after the horses and keeping the ranches always looking amazing. For the times I missed a birthday, a play, or a school function, I am the luckiest person alive with the family I have.

TABLE OF CONTENTS

Author Notes

This book idea was created at a Friday's restaurant in May 2003. I had this idea for a book about my experiences with family businesses and discussed it with a great friend, Peter Fisher, to see if he would like the concept and the challenge of this project.

I was recently unemployed because a great businessman had decided that his son should run the business. That son felt he did not need any experienced senior management to help him run the show. In his mind, the company only needed him. He was part of the lucky sperm club, so I quickly found myself surplus to requirements. In the months following, many executive managers of this business were also let go as they were no longer seen as "needed." I witnessed many friends lose their jobs, and all the hard work we had accomplished was spiraling down the toilet.

With time on my hands, looking for the next step in my future, and having a friend like Peter to bounce ideas off,

I conceived this book and realized there were tons of stories out there just like mine begging to be told.

I would like to thank all my mentors, employees, and managers who have worked for me over the years; I would not be where I am today if it was not for them. This book has been produced for some great colleagues, and I would like to thank them all personally for supporting this project and telling me stories about where they worked or used to work.

I discovered while working with or talking to companies and their employees, many subjects and wanted to present the funniest and the best of the best in this book. It has taken me more than sixteen years to finish this collection. As I started the project, I took on a new position at a company and placed this on hold again and again. My goal is to make this an easy read, something to take on a plane. I flew forty-eight weeks a year for over eighteen years and was always looking for some fun and entertaining reads for a laugh. I hope after reading this book, you will take it back to your company for further discussion with managers and employees. I, therefore, hope you find it both entertaining and useful.

MDE

CHAPTER 1

A Company Run by God and Owned by the Devils

This story concerns a company founded in the late 1970s and located somewhere on the East Coast. It was a family-owned business run by the father and his sons. As you'll see, it isn't always a brilliant idea to keep it in the family...

I worked for a manufacturing company that built all types of equipment for various markets. They reached success with the first product they launched in the late 1970s, an out-of-the-box design that no one had or ever thought of, which exploded into the marketplace like the Pet Rock when it was launched.

This product took over the market, and the sales came in daily. It took little to no effort to sell this product. There was no need to be a sales or marketing professional -- you just needed to know how to write a person's name and information down and take a 50% deposit with a lead time of up to six months. As the first ten years passed, everything went fantastically well in terms of finances. The cash flowed into the bank faster than the Colorado River, and business went unbelievably well.

The owners of this company claimed to have Christian beliefs and hired employees with views that aligned with their own. If you were an accountant by trade and needed a job, you could definitely fill the shoes of the engineering position looking to be filled if your belief aligned. No experience needed! You would quickly become an engineer overnight.

This is how they staffed the company, and they did not care if you had the knowledge and passion for the job or the company. The key was this -- talk about God and pray at lunch, and you would be employed for life. Please don't take this the wrong way. These people were great; however, some did not have the skills to be in the position they were hired.

This company was founded by an amazing man who cared about people, his church, and his community. His wife was an even better person than him. He had been a manager of a successful company before starting this business with his sons. The problem wasn't him. The problem was the boys. He and his wife had only boys, and each one of them came with a huge ego—they were brothers, but never friends.

This was a family who preached the word of God, yet in their own house, they would not even talk to each other. At one charity event, this became evident as the father and his sons sat at different tables. The sons and father had not purchased separate tables; however, they refused to sit with one another or converse with each other throughout the night.

Ten years passed, and they all began to have money of their own to spend. That's when the greed erupted. Please remember, they did give their share to charities and the local community, but still, they wanted more. The company, off the top, gave 15% toward charities, missions, schools, you name it; they had a full-time charity department to pass out the money. The only problem was that it needed to be for God, such as a mission trip, or something the owners wanted to give money to that specific charity. The funds were not meant to help the employees if there was a death in the family, etc. They had a profit-sharing program but would use it as a salary when they hired you, so you would not make a great deal over one year, essentially making it a scam to hire new employees.

For example, if the industry average for an account level 1 were $58,000 a year, they would pay an employee a base of $48,000 with a monthly profit share of 30%, ultimately making the employee $62,400 for the year. However, the profit-sharing could go away at any time.

Here is some background on the family. The father was a humble man and drove an average car, which was five years old. His wife was the same way. She was also a mother to all and made everyone around her feel special. This family lived in a beautiful house, yet it was not too extreme. They traveled for mission work all around the world and always flew coach. They were not flashy dressers, did not flaunt their money, and housed missionaries for months at a time when they needed a place to stay.

They expected you would do the same when working for the company -- drive a lower-class car, dress in casual clothing, and not discuss the things you have.

The oldest son was a total geek. To paint a picture for you, he was 5'10," weighed 190 pounds, and assumed he was better than everyone, which became apparent as he talked down to those around him. Let's just say sports was a six-letter word to him. He bought every kind of gadget that came out. He was a loner and did not like to make friends. I tried for years to become his friend, and it became clear that this wouldn't happen. As a result, he was always jealous of his younger brother, the one with the looks, the one who was earning more money, and the one who was smarter and could motivate anyone who was around him. This son, we'll call him Bob, was the leader, the thinker and the one who became the President & CEO. This always made the oldest brother mad and upset. One day he decided to go and work in one of the manufacturing operations overseas. He told his wife he would be there for roughly a week and then stayed for the next twelve years. The older brother divorced his wife, left his kids, and married someone else.

Bob, the son with all the brains, was always under his father's eye. Dad would not let this son manage the business like it needed to be operated. The father hired middle to lower managers to run departments, and there was no one in the family, except Bob, who liked to bring in staff with passion, drive, and expertise in management. So, they ended up with managers who hated it when anyone asked any questions. As a result, Bob, in the early 1990s, had enough and left the business to form a new company that he would go on to make successful.

Son number three was the closet son, the one who had great ideas but always had to beg his father and brothers to put these ideas into action. In some respect, he was the smartest one of all because he just did his own thing and did not make waves. He was a hard worker and had some big dreams. However, in the end, he cost the company a lot of dollars, and did not challenge his older brother.

The last son was the baby who was in the family business for only a few years. He was spoiled rotten, mom always bailed him out, and he wasted everything away the company gave to him. He was never a factor in the business, fortunately.

This story came to me as I worked for them for a few years in an executive position, and I quickly learned that this family business lived to preach the Word of God and promote Christian values. Yet they did not follow them. All the sons, but one, have divorced at least once. Some have been involved in drugs, sexual harassment, cheating on their wives, and there were various scandals in which mom and dad ensured that all the employees remained silent. When

I was hired, I was told that God managed the company, and then a few months later, I figured it out it was owned by the Devil.

When I started the job, I moved from the Southeast to the East Coast to manage one of their divisions, with a lot of promises and goodwill suggesting that this would be a job for life and would reap me great rewards. It was in the late 1990s, and Bob, the smart son, had already left to start his own business. It was successful, and dad and Bob had a discussion and came to the conclusion that the original company would purchase Bob's company; dad would retire, and Bob would become the CEO. This was a great idea, and Bob was excited to do this.

I remember my first day at work. The retired dad came into my office and introduced himself, talking to me for five minutes. The main thing that came out of his mouth was along the lines of, "You are a manager in one of my companies, and I better never hear that you're at a strip bar or out drinking with your staff." Then he shook my hand and walked away -- what a warm "Welcome to the company" that was.

With Bob as CEO, the fun was about to begin. Bob was an out-of-the-box thinker, and his ideas were different from those of the rest of the family. First, he wanted to break up each division and make them run as profit centers, letting each manager run his individual division and see if he would sink or swim. Bob was the kind of person who, when he walked into the room and started to talk, would have everyone listening to him.

I was about eight months into the job when Bob contacted me and offered a position to manage one of his divisions. I first spoke to him on a Wednesday, he flew me in on a Saturday morning, and that same Saturday afternoon offered me the position. As we had dinner on Saturday night, I was told he would fax me a proposal on Monday.

Monday soon came and went. Along came Tuesday, and I had a call from Steve, one of the other division managers, who advised me Bob was no longer CEO and that he, himself, would be taking over. The next day, Steve asked me to fly back that following weekend to finalize my contract and meet some staff.

That weekend, Steve was there to pick me up at the airport. The new CEO arranged a meeting with me and some other executives. The meetings went well, and they would have a contract for me by Monday. I accepted the position and was due to start two weeks later.

At this point, all I could think was, *So far, so good*, and *I'm excited to be here*.

This is where the fun begins.

I remember my first day on the job. The retired father pranced into my office and introduced himself. We talked for about five minutes. The moral of the conversation we shared was explicitly expressed when he stated, "You are a manager in one of my companies, and I will never hear that you're at a strip club or out drinking with your staff. Got it?" He proceeded to give me a firm handshake and swiftly walked away.

I was running a business, something I had dreamed of doing all my life. My family had just moved to be with me, when about four months in, the father called me into a board meeting. He and Bob had just had another fight, and he advised me that they were selling my division. The next four months were spent working on a project and attempting to keep the news from my staff, as advised by the board.

Bob's original company had recently cost $12 million, and we received an offer for $26 million. However, the father said, "No, we wanted thirty million." Negotiations went on and off for two years. One minute we were selling, the next we weren't. It started driving the board, my family, their family, and me crazy. What was keeping me going was that every year my business sales were growing 20% and increasing the profit to the main corporation. My division was the shining star of the whole company as we grew the product line, developed new dealers, and expanded both the planned operations and the international business.

While I was employed, I was making fantastic money and had hired the staff I wanted to work alongside and lead. Between them, they had over fifty years of experience in the business, plus we were all friends. We had common goals -- grow the sales, be the best, and show the world how we could make this company shine in the industry.

It didn't take too long for the board of directors to leave me alone with my staff and allow me to grow the business. They gave me the tools I needed to be successful. After a year, in which we'd come off a record sales year, the father called all the executives into a meeting and advised the board to let Steve, the current CEO, go, and that his oldest son, Bill, was now to be the new CEO who we all would report. This was the first time in my life that I'd worked for someone and felt I lost control of everything I had been working on for years. This son was a prick; no one enjoyed being around him when he came to town. He had destroyed everything he touched in business and life, and he was gunning for a lot of us who worked at this company.

The very day the news about Bill becoming CEO was broken to us was the day I was called into the father's office and told I would be moving to corporate and managing all the division sales. In this closed-door meeting, with only the father, I was told that Bill and I would be the ones to sign off on everything. When I asked if this was alright with Bill, I didn't receive a response. I thought to myself, *Oh, crap! This will be tons of fun.*

As I said, Bill had been based overseas for some twelve years. On his return, at one of our first meetings, he advised me that everyone in the U.S. was lazy and overpaid and that he was going to change this. His solution was to bring in overseas employees to do what he considered excessive management jobs. Once again, I thought, *Oh, crap!*

As time went by, you could see this guy was a loner, had no friends, and that he had no intention of making any. I would ask if he wanted to grab dinner or lunch but always received a sharp, "No." Bill had no desire to be a team member or friend. He pushed people away and had no respect for anyone. I can still remember being in a meeting with some executives when we discussed the state of the company. About a third of the way through, Bill turned to his laptop and wrote e-mails with his back to us all. Every time we would ask him a question, he would say, "What?!" Then we would have to ask the same question again, just to see if he would answer.

This son had the idea for every manager to watch John Maxwell's management tapes. At the end of the day, this was actually one of the best programs I have ever attended. To this day, I recommend these tapes to every company. In one tape, John Maxwell talked about being at an executive meeting. He mentioned that if you were the CEO, and it was time to discuss engineering and your background was accounting, then you should pass the baton to the engineering manager, and he would become the CEO for this section. The executive staff loved this part of the program.

Please remember, Bill had made us watch these tapes each week and advised us to learn from them. There was only one problem -- when it was time to pass the CEO baton, he would simply not let go! We would pull and tug, and not once would he let go. After this, it was hard to motivate the staff by the tapes or even care what John Maxwell had to say. This was a shame and a waste of twenty hours per manager— that's 2,000 total company management hours.

Before we continue with the story about Bill, I have a question for you. Where were you on 9/11? I will never forget. I was overseas at one of our operations with four executives and the CEO, Bill, who was there with his family when the news came in about the attacks. The one thing we will never understand is how he reacted to the impact of 9/11. Where we were, the news covered it only a couple of minutes every hour, and no one spent so much time thinking about the U.S. being attacked; they just went on with their own business. We were in a country that spoke very little English, and U.S. executives had no one to communicate with aside from each other.

This is when I found out what a leader the son became. His first comment was, "This is a great place to be stuck," and that he did not want to go home, anyway. Then as we worked for days trying to get some information or a flight home, he turned up and told us he'd found a flight for himself and his family and that he was leaving the next day. "Good luck," he told us, "don't spend a lot of dollars getting home."

Just like that, we were on our own to figure out what to do. Imagine if General Patton said this to his soldiers in the field. We all had been overseas for over ten days, had no clothes left, money was running low, and we were staying in a dump that smelled like an old dog. What I will say is that the staff of this company was amazing. They would do anything to ensure that we felt safe. I will never forget that day, or week, both for the impact on the country I call home, and because I learned what kind of leader we were working for.

I remember a specific product meeting we had with Bill. He asked what we were selling the product for. I did some costing on one of the products and found that we were selling a unit to our overseas dealers at a rate below our manufacturing costs. As I brought this up in the executive meeting, the CEO informed me that I was crazy and didn't know what I was talking about. That is when the CFO of the company spoke up and said that the number I was stating was correct and that we were losing dollars each time we sold this product. This didn't even count the warranty expense each unit would have over the subsequent year or so. The CEO then told us both we did not know what we were talking about and that he was the boss. Essentially, we were told to "Shut up and do it his way."

Each sale was losing the company over $6000 per unit. By the end of his first year as CEO, the company had lost over $2 million in net profit and was down $8 million in net profit over the year before sales. I had come across many items we would develop and sell with an excessive cost that no one was willing to discuss.

What did this mean to the managers and employees who, for over the last twenty years, had received a fantastic bonus check each month and year? Now the bonus program was canceled, and it was cost-cutting time.

A meeting was called with the CEO, CFO, HR-VP, HR Manager, and myself to discuss letting employees go for the first time in the history of the company. Plus, with the bonus gone, employees were making less and less. Some had even decided to leave.

The first thing to cut, in the CEO's eyes, was the VP of Marketing. This VP was a visionary and had some fantastic ideas. He would always present new products to sell, which would ultimately grow the business, so the whole executive team pleaded with him not to do this. As the CEO asked this person to leave, we asked him what the plan was. He did not have one.

Next thing we knew, Bill had put a low-level manager in that position, someone who was not qualified to manage a popcorn stand. I went into his office and told him this would not work, and then I brought this up with the board who advised me to stay out of it. However, I'd called it right on the button -- first projects fell behind, then there were no timelines, shows were missing marketing materials, there were no new marketing ideas, and sales started to plummet. The crazy part was that some stockholders even went to the chairman (dad, if you'll remember) and told him the company desperately needed some change. He would just say that the CEO was doing a great job.

The next big project for the CEO was to open an operation in Japan. We asked what we were going to do over there, and he told us we needed to build cheaper products so we could sell our products in that market. Soon enough, he marched right to the board, sold them on this, and built a $2 million building. The big problem was that nobody had done a business plan to project what kind of market there was. A main question was, "Who would manage the business?"

First, there were tons of people to work in the new business, but none had the funds to purchase the inventory to build products. Then, there was no plan when it came to what product to build. This uncertainty went on for a year, and by the end of it, the company was still not building anything, just spending company dollars. This project ended up costing the company a further $1 million a year or so just to be dormant.

Then the CEO decided to let go of the VP of Sales. This person was the backbone of the company; he brought passion and knew how to motivate others, had a mind of his own, and knew how to execute projects successfully. The CEO did not like him because the staff respected him, and went to him with ideas, suggestions, and to raise their problems, rather than to the CEO. This was a hard blow to company morale, and staff members of all kinds went to the CEO and advised him not to do this. Now the company had no-one with great sales experience, ideas, passion, or an understanding of the true business. The CEO moved sales managers into the position; they were great guys but had been thrown to the wolves and needed a mentor to support them. Nobody could, and no other departments could help them either.

As the next few months passed, sales were crashing faster than ever. One of the new sales managers started to fire some of his sales staff the second they challenged his management style and ideas. These were employees that were well known in the industry. Then he made a terrible move; he staffed the open positions with rookies. When a big problem arose, all the new management, and the CEO himself, did not know what to do. They would fall flat on their face in front of the customer. They kept coming up with excuses that it was the old VP's fault and did their best to spread this rumor through the industry, the company, and the owners.

Six months later, one of the replacement sales managers was let go. Bill replaced him with a friend who had a computing background. This new employee was hired to manage sales in an equipment company.

I could go on forever, but the short story is that sales kept decreasing.

The next executive to go was the VP of IT. This person was the glue of this department, and he worked six days a week and cared about the company like it was his own. He would work extra hours just to help any department reach its goal. The CEO moved one of the former VP's staff up into his position, and the same thing started to happen -- jobs fell behind, no department support... you name it.

That was the end of the terrible firing decisions. Next out was the VP of Manufacturing. He had been with the company from the start, and he knew everything about it from top to bottom. Of course, the CEO brought one of his boys from overseas to manage manufacturing. This guy was a nice fellow, but his experience was as a low-level manager, and a few months later, Bill was even talking about firing him. This poor new VP was paddling upstream without a paddle from day one.

We're not done with the disastrous moves. The CFO was next out the door. He was another employee who had worked like he was one of the owners, six days a week, twelve hours a day, advising the board about everything. Bill felt that this guy was not a team player and asked him to leave. Additionally, the CFO had advised all the stock members of what was going on with the company, why they were losing money, and what they needed to do, but the CEO and the owners would not adapt to his ideas. Two years in a row with millions lost on ROI and with corporate sales crashing, over 50% of sales were lost, and distributors had started giving up on selling our products or ordering from us.

No one wanted to hear this, and the board agreed with the CEO to let the CFO go. The CEO still blamed the poor VP of Sales, always telling everyone that he had sold too much product in the field and over-stocked the market. Losing the CFO was probably his biggest mistake ever.

The HR of Engineering was let go alongside managers from different departments who had been employed by the company for years.

The last to go was the VP of HR. He was the keeper of the culture and was a people person. He was a great man and cared about all the employees and their wellbeing. Of his own accord, he found a great position elsewhere, where he'd wanted to work all his life. He left on his own before the CEO got rid of him.

At this point, the CEO had replaced the whole executive team and all the guys who had been new to the company. The company that once made such great ROI was left with under-experienced staff. Bill had removed any company vision or five-year plan from the table. The

CEO had merged all parts of the business. The manager of manufacturing was the manager of all the departments. The company had locations everywhere, yet no one in charge had experience leading multiple locations and product lines. Still, Bill advised the board, "Now watch and see what I can do with my staff."

Four months in, the corporation was looking at another year of at least $3 million loss, with sales continuing to plummet.

Bob, the number two brother who had been out of the company for a while, stepped in and called an emergency board meeting. The board decided to make some changes. The father resigned as chairman, Bob became the new CEO, and the eldest son became the COO. This lasted for about one month until Bob sent his brother packing back to the overseas operation from where he'd come.

So, when you talk about being in the lucky sperm club, this son certainly was a leading member. However, he eventually got what he deserved, and so did the corporation because they had decided not to listen to anyone but the number one son. The values of the company were lost, and I do not know if they will ever come back. The money and market share that was lost is gone for good and would be difficult to recoup. Sadly, although the son that destroyed the corporation had lost millions, fired some great managers, and terminated 150 employees, he still had a job. He moved back overseas, resigned from the board, after being asked to, and left the family to pick up the pieces. The CEO had the family sell their stock in ESP to the employees to try to put things back together.

In the end, he won. The employees and the company lost... and he returned to where he had wanted to be in the first place.

It must be nice to be in the sperm club.

Let's discuss this chapter. The business was successful, had amazing team members, and a product any business would dream of having available. So, where did they go wrong? Have your team read this chapter and discuss the business with them. Take time to bond your team together, while having laughs along the way, and by discussing this chapter together.

Thanks for the story. This one is for the executive team that was let go.

CHAPTER 2

Why Could My Last Name Not Be Jones?

This is a story about a family business from late 2008. Personally, this wasn't an experience I had, yet one I was told about anonymously. The story comes from the manager of a family-owned chain of restaurants who had three Italian pasta shops in Los Angeles and around Southern California.

As the regional manager for the restaurant chain, I worked directly for the mother. The father had passed away three years before I started, and the mother was the backbone of the company. She had put in years of hard work and long hours to make this chain successful. As a result, it was very well-known and very profitable.

I had been involved in the restaurant business for seventeen years, and the mother contacted me to discuss a position managing the restaurants for her. This was a great opportunity for me, and she needed some help. In my interview, I asked her, "What about your son?" She informed me that he was a waste of space, spent most of his time on the beach, and would not be involved in the business.

With hopes high, I took the position. From day one, things were looking up for me. I helped sales reach an all-time high, and the costs were low. Soon enough, the mother had given me a bonus that brought tears to my eyes.

Just after my second year with the company, when sales were at an all-time high, and net profits were off the charts, the mother called me into her office to discuss a new plan for her company. She told me that her son was turning thirty on Friday, and he was ready to take over the business. The mother believed that he had cleaned up his act and that a family member needed to be involved. Needless to say, I was confused by this. By this point, I had seen enough of him to completely support the assessment of him she had given me in my interview. Yet, I took the time to hear her out, and I told her I supported her decision. She stepped back from running the business full-time, and in he came.

The first few weeks were fine with the son, and he let me do my work and manage the employees, and business was going great. This was a business that the employees enjoyed working at. It was as if we were a big family driving the train down the tracks of success.

A few months later, I was called into a meeting by the son, and he informed me that he was going to change the menu. As this raised some questions, I asked, "Why?"

He told me that we needed younger people to come to our restaurants. The thing is, most of our restaurants were in the business districts of LA. Our customers were professionals who took their clients out for lunch and dinner. Because of this, we were upscale, with tablecloths, fine wines, and great food.

The son's first change was to change the look of the restaurant to target a younger crowd. We brought in surfboards, new menus, colored tables, and our service staff were to be outfitted with swim apparel to wear while serving the customers. This huge change led to a loss of employees as menu prices dropped, and their tips decreased. In the thirty days following this change, sales had gone down 26%, and the net profit was down 14%.

Next, I was told to hire younger employees and make sure they were tan and had the bodies of supermodels and fitness professionals. His "helpful tip" was to go to the beach to find employees. With concern, I asked the son about restaurant skills, and he informed me that they wouldn't need them. The new brand was to look great, and this would bring the customers in.

I ran an ad online and in the local paper, and I actually did go to the beach to hand out our "help wanted" ad. Within the first week, we received 125 resumes. Most of the responses were from women nineteen to twenty-six, who looked great but had no restaurant experience. As I started to hire employees and let the old staff go, we could see problems mounting. If you can't trust your staff, business is going to suffer. One problem after the other began to pile up. Orders would be placed wrong; it took more staff to cover the same number of tables, and the net effect was that costs were rising with lower sales and net profits.

It was about four months into all the changes, and I was called into the office again. This time I was told that Kelly, a long-time employee, was being a problem, and that I had to fire her. My first thought was to suggest a few ways we could help her improve. Yet, I was simply told, "Do this or leave."

That night I let Kelly go. This infuriated the staff, and at this point, it had become nearly impossible to please the employees. One week later, I was called in again and was told to fire Brenda, another long-standing employee. Just like the first experience, I suggested ways to help Brenda. However, I was told to "Just do it." Something just did not feel right with the whole situation, but I acceded to his requests. Sales continued to drop, and the staff failed to show up for shifts. There was not much left to do.

Before long, I was told that the son would close more often and that I just needed to work day shifts. This didn't make sense to me. When you manage restaurants, you need to be there for the peak shifts, so I asked him how I was supposed to manage the business this way. Again, he just said that this was my new shift pattern, and that this was how it was going to be from now on.

After one month in my new shift schedule, the business had hit an all-time low, sales were down 39%, and for the first time since I had been employed there, we were losing money. One night I found myself out at dinner in the neighborhood. The restaurant I was at was now staffed with many of our previous employees. We had a fun time filled with both fantastic service and food. I happened to pass by the restaurant I worked at and thought I saw someone inside, so I decided to take a look at what was happening. This was not normal because the restaurant should have been closed by then, so my inner alarm bells went off. I stopped, turned off the alarm, and looked inside.

First, I noticed the son was there; then I heard a scream. I unlocked the front door and rushed to the kitchen and could not believe my eyes. The son had Julie, another long-time employee, on the counter, telling her to take her clothes off. He was yelling at her. His demands were that if she did not perform sexual acts on him, she would be fired. Julie was a single mother and needed this job. As I looked into Julie's eyes, I realized that she seemed as if she were not "all there." It was as if she had been drugged as her head was bobbing up and down.

Needless to say, this was tremendously sickening. Honestly, I could not believe my eyes and I stood there frozen in my tracks for a second. I yelled out to the son, "Stop! What's going on?" and I walked over to Julie, who was stumbling on her words and glossy-eyed.

The son said, "You better leave, or you're fired." Then he pushed me away from Julie. With a knife in hand, he said, "Get out now!"

Soon enough, he grabbed my wrist. This was the moment I looked at him and hit him as hard as I could and with one punch. I laid him out cold. My brain was in a fog, but I do remember that he was out cold. He was just lying there, not moving, blood all over his shirt. I thought, "Wow, not a bad punch."

Once, I would have said nobody should have ever reacted this way, but when I was threatened, and so was Julie, he had it coming to him.

I grabbed Julie and said, "Let's go," and I took her to the police station. The next day the police came and arrested the son and I gave my resignation to the mother.

I advised her of all of my concerns, but of course, a mother could only believe her son and she said, "He'd never do anything like that." As a mom, she was believed her son could do no wrong. The even worse part, the police informed us that he had a record of violence in the past. Within the next few weeks, I spoke to several employees who still worked there. They informed me that things were continuing to spiral downward. The mother tried to work at the restaurant. However, all hope was lost as the reputation for this place was now terrible.

A mother's love. That is all I can say.

Since then, months have passed by and I recently drove by one of the restaurants, only to see a "For Lease" sign on the window. The place was locked up and closed. All I could think about was the fact that one person could bring down something so good, so fast.

The rest is history. All of them are now closed or have been sold, and I was told the mother left town.

Thanks for that story, anonymous contributor from Los Angeles.

CHAPTER 3

Working for Eeyore

Have you ever worked for Eeyore? Think back to your days as a child, reading "Winnie the Pooh." Think of Eeyore the donkey, how he talked, how he walked, and how he always had that negative attitude. As you read about the CEO in this chapter, keep Eeyore in mind.

I worked for a company on the East Coast as a director of sales, marketing, and operations. We were a distributor selling supplies, tractors, grass seed, and other products to golf courses, contractors, parks and recreation facilities, cities, schools, and sports complexes.

I joined this company in the early 1990s. They had been in business for over sixty years and management were in their third generation. Back in the day, at the start of the company, they were the leaders in the industry but with changes in business, costs were rising and the family did not want to invest further into the business—they just wanted their share of the profits each year. As time went by, they had lost a major market share and it was time for dad to retire.

As I have seen many times in my business career, dad stepped down and decided it was time for his lucky sperm club member (or son/daughter) to take charge. This time around, the son was a smart person. However, like most CEOs (Children Employed by Owners), his son had no real-life experience. Living by the silver spoon rule, he had only ever worked in the office, had not spent time with his customers, was out of touch with the business trends, and truly did not understand what this business was all about.

We are going to call this CEO Eeyore because his passion and temperament were pretty much the same. He came to work each day with a negative attitude, always down, wanting to please his father, and did not like working in the company, but where else was he going to go? He would fight with his wife and then take it out on the employees. His problem was that he did not know the right thing to say to the right person. He liked to stir things up with his manufacturers, and they hated to do business with him. When he took the reins as CEO, the problems started -- sales crashed, he could not keep the staff, and the cash flow was gone. Plus, he wouldn't hire the best of the best, yet settle on someone who did not truly know the position. One of his major product lines told him that he had to hire someone to help manage the business and to help turn the company around, as it had been in the red for the past four years and was on its way to losing their biggest manufacturer.

Eeyore was a good person inside; he did care about people and his staff, but he just did not know how to show it. Eventually, the staff was showing up looking like zombies. Some days I think he had a goal to see who he could make cry. He could take a salesperson that had just walked in feeling positive, having received a great order, and before they could drop the order off and were ready to move onto the next account, Eeyore would have something to say.

"The margins are not high enough!" or, "You gave everything away!" or, "Why did you not get all the orders?" were phrases that would regularly spew out of his mouth. By the time the salesperson left the office, he would be so mad and upset he would just go home, or straight into the next account with such a bad attitude that the customer would lose respect for them. The number one goal when managing sales staff is to keep them positive, even if this means stroking their egos.

This is where I came in. I had been working for a manufacturer and when calling on some accounts in Eeyore's distributor territory, we met for lunch. Eeyore asked if I would come and work for his company. When trying to hire someone he was as good as it gets; he did actually know how to read people and what they wanted to hear. Yet, he did not use this skill enough in day-to-day business. We discussed the position he was looking to fill and came to an agreement, months later, that I would run the sales department and had the authority to make changes and bring in the staff I needed to complete the task in hand. This meant that I could let everyone go and do some major restructuring if needed.

I had been told stories about Eeyore and everyone warned me that this wouldn't be a great move. Yet, when

I was around him, he put this great face on, and I found myself eager to work for him. It appeared that he did genuinely want someone to make big changes and was ready to let some responsibilities go.

The first few months were like most new positions in a new company; I was in the honeymoon phase. I could truly do no wrong. As I developed a plan for each department and staff member, and worked on a strategic plan to turn the fortunes of the company around and for us to become the leaders in the industry, I found the "Do Not Touch Syndrome" existed in each department. There were employees who did not know their job, some who should never have been hired in that position ever, some were family members, and some who were just the good old boys. You know, the type of people you hear about when you hear things like this, "Yeah, Joe? He's just been here forever. Why not just let him be?" The problem was that Bruce was a snake in the ground and liked to cause problems with everyone on any given day.

As the months passed by, I started to hire the staff I needed and let the ones go that should have never been there in the first place. I had sales personnel who liked to sit in the office and drink coffee all morning, only to start their day around 10:00 a.m. Then they would drive for an hour before they would even be in their sales territory. When I confronted them, they would tell me that this was how they had done business for over ten years. They would explain that Eeyore wanted them to check in first, to make sure they were working that day. I asked them what their cell phone was for, and each of them replied along the lines of, "I was told not to use it unless it was an emergency."

Keep in mind that this was back in the day when cell phone charges were by the minute. Additionally, there was no texting or emailing. If you wanted to reach someone, you would use their calling card. For those of you reading this that are too young to know what that is, take that to the Internet and find out!

I discussed this with Eeyore, and he told me, "We're not going to have these huge phone bills just for them to check in once in a while." So, instead, his solution was to have those salespeople coming into the office and losing two to three hours a day at $100 an hour. In today's market, this would be costing the team about $250 an hour.

I would ask, "What is your plan for the week?" to the sales staff and they would say, "For the week? I don't even have a plan for today."

"What do you mean?" I would ask.

They informed me that Eeyore wanted to come in each day and tell them whom they were going to see, and then he would let them know if this would work for the day. Ultimately, every sales visit had to pass the CEO's approval.

Another problem they had was that they had to keep an eye on gas prices. If gas was high that week or even that day, they were told they had better not travel too far, as it was not in the budget. So, it was easier to sit in the office and do nothing.

When I asked Eeyore about this, he responded by questioning, "What is the sales staff talking about? Gas is not in the budget."

I later learned that they budgeted gas at $2.00 a gallon and currently gas was at $2.30 a gallon, so this is not in the budget. "They do not need to travel so many miles each day, anyway."

I asked Eeyore, "How do we achieve sales if the team is in the office all day long and do not call on customers?"

He responded, "That is why we have telephones."

The thing is, we were in the supply business and our customers would not purchase products from us if they did not have the chance to see the product or try it out. Every day spent entirely on the phones was another wasted day. The problem was not the fact that people were on the phone, the problem was that days and hours were wasted by speaking on the phone rather than giving customers that chance to try the product out.

This was just the start. Next door to us was the service department, and we had a service manager who looked like a rock n' roll star and did not like to get dirty, talk on the phone, discuss problems with customers, or do a shred of paperwork. When I confronted Eeyore about this, he informed me, "Sam is okay, just leave him alone."

Here we go again with a service manager issue. If service is not up to par, the goal of making customers happy seems to be unattainable.

However, when the end of the month rolled around, I would ask Eeyore, "Why is your service department losing dollars?"

In reply he asked me, "Why are there no warranty claims or service jobs being billed this month?" and would continue with, "You need to get on this right away!"

I quickly read into what was happening. The service manager was not doing anything, and this was soon to change with my leadership.

We had our company branches review, and each one had a branch manager with sales staff, a parts department, and a service department. When I asked,

"What do you do all day?" to each branch manager, they simply told me they managed the branch. I asked, "Do you ever go see accounts?" and they all said they did not. I asked why and they advised me that Eeyore told them that they needed to be in the branch to manage their operations. I asked, "What if it is slow and no one is doing anything—why not go call on some accounts?"

They told me that they did not have a car or truck to drive and that Eeyore would not pay those miles or gas to use their own vehicle. Again, all this was to change in the coming months.

I would go to the branches weekly and look at the costs of some four to six people sitting around, and I would ask, "What is this costing us, to do nothing?" The room would fall silent as no one would answer.

Amazingly, the branch manager was paid on all sales, and when I asked him, "Where do you make more money, sitting in the office or paying for some gas out of your own pocket to create more sales?"

He was dumbfounded. Honestly, he just did not understand that the more sales that came in, the more money he would make. Also, it's worth noting that this was back in the day when there was no requirement by state law to pay employees for the money they spent on gas.

Back to the sales personnel who were all driving company trucks that were at least six years old with the newest one having 135,000 miles. This was a problem because the sales personnel were scared to drive too far away from the office or their house in case they broke down and got stuck somewhere.

I started to look at the sales call reports and discovered that most of the sales staff had over two hundred accounts. Yet, they only called on thirty accounts each month and they were always the same accounts -- the ones we call the "good old boy of coffee" accounts. These were the kind of accounts you'd go to and have coffee with Jim each day; though Jim never purchased anything because he had no budget, but he was such a great guy and he always made you feel good.

Eventually, I asked Eeyore, "Why haven't you discussed this problem with each salesperson over the years? Do you have these on itineraries and call reports?" At this point in time, there were no CRM's.

He informed me that he'd never read them, that his dad had always made the sales staff track their reports and place them on a spreadsheet, but that he hadn't liked that job, so he just filed them away in a folder each week.

I couldn't believe that he hadn't looked into any of the practices or working methods of his sales team. I questioned him, "How did you manage the staff and advise them on their territory?"

His reply was, "I told them to go sell and if they did not have an order, I got rid of them."

Now, this company was doing sales of four million in a market that had a total sales potential of forty-five million in sales each year. With competition getting harder and many products on the market, and the margins decreasing, you had to become more creative, which meant no longer worrying about the ROI on each sale, but the actual dollars each sale would bring in.

This is typically a problem for most CEOs, especially the ones who come from an accounting background and not a sales background. Therefore, I love to discuss this aspect in particular with accountants: we had two products, one selling for five thousand and the other one for forty thousand. Both units needed to go to the service department to be set up and receive a PDI (pre-delivery inspection) before delivery. They each had a list price with a GPM (gross profit margin) of thirty percent and each took less than one hour for the PDI to be completed and to be ready for delivery.

Eeyore would not let the sales team sell for less than twenty-six percent or they had to lose the sale. They'd sell ten a year of the forty thousand units.

My words to Eeyore were, "We sell both units to the same accounts, and they take the same time to PDI and deliver. If we sell the units at five thousand per unit, this will bring us in a GPM of seventeen hundred at a twenty-six percent margin and if we sell the forty thousand unit at twenty-six percent gross profit margin, it will bring in nine thousand. But if we lower our price to a few thousand we will sell between thirty to fifty units and instead of making ninety thousand for the year on this one product we would make three hundred and twenty thousand plus. That's just extra sales, without any more time, or resources, required from the service department for delivery costs."

Eeyore's answer was, "But you're taking our gross profit margin down and this is what I forecasted to the bank. If the bank sees us drop the gross profit margin like this, then they will question me."

It took months before I could get Eeyore to understand that he should have been looking at dollars per sale and not gross profit margin. This is a good way to bankrupt any distributor.

The resemblance between this Eeyore and the Eeyore we all know was uncanny. Each morning Eeyore would come to the office and walk in, just like in the "Winnie the Pooh" stories.

You would say, "Good morning, how are you doing? Is this not a great day?"

You would inevitably get the same response, "What is so great?" (And remember to read this very slowly like Eeyore would speak, "Whaaaaaaat is sooooo greaaaaat?").

He would move like a snail and trudge into his office and wait until the mail arrived. If the receivables were good that day, he would loosen up some. We called that a Code Two. If they were great, he would even buy lunch. That was a Code Three, and it was a good day to talk to him. But if they were low or nothing came in, well that pity party was known as a Code One. It was usually fine for me as I would grab my keys and go call on some accounts. But the poor office staff was stuck all day hearing the complaints.

My main job was to be the cheerleader, to keep the morale up, and to keep the staff selling. The best thing that ever happened to distribution was a company called Nextel. They provided these cell phones with two-way radios. If I was in the office and the receivables were low that day, I would step out back and call each sales personnel and say, "Do not come into the office today unless you have to -- we are having a Code One."

I would then go out and see one of the branches and before I headed back to the corporate office, I would call my assistant and ask how the day was going. She would tell me whether it was a Code One, Two, or Three. If it was a Three, that was time to go in and ask for something I needed to make the company run more efficiently... And that trick is how I had to operate to make that company more successful. We made a tremendous amount of changes within the first year. Sales increased, money was coming in, and the team was becoming a team that all worked towards the same goal.

Then the fun really began... How would one rebuild this company with Eeyore in charge? I decided to do it my way and work with the staff to increase the sales numbers. If possible, we were not going to lose any more sales. I did restructure the team and brought in some top sales executives, then worked on each branch manager. They all received a territory of their own and learned not to sit in the office but to go see accounts. Then the service department was restructured, and a new service manager was hired, and the most important person hired was a parts manager who could give the sales staff after-market support. Finally, I had the staff in place and a plan of action.

In the first year we increased sales by fifty percent, year two by thirty-five percent, and year three by twenty-eight percent. We then continued with nice increases for the next six years. The sales increase was great but more awesome was the return on investment "ROI." We went from losing five hundred thousand a year to making money the first year.

It just became better each year after that. The staff, management, and owners won trips for different manufacturers, prizes, and awards. We received new trucks, trailers, and clothes, which branded our company name. Soon enough, we were the talk of the town and the talk of the business industry. We would receive calls asking how this was done or whether we had any openings. When we'd attend shows, meetings, or manufacturing functions, they would talk about us. This was the best high I'd ever had in my life and I felt that there was only room for growth. At this point, I had companies asking me to work with their staff and help train them to be successful.

Then it happened.

Eeyore was getting a big head and started to buck my ideas and the systems and process I had in place. He hated that the staff would come to me with their problems and he felt he had lost his power. The tension was getting to me and I knew it was time to go. Ultimately, I had the reputation of being a problem solver and the go-to man and was also called the

"Rainmaker." I was offered positions from two companies and I decided it was time to move on.

It was a good time to go, but I also felt hurt. I had placed a fantastic team together that was like my family and it felt as if I was leaving to go to college or join the army. I did not want to go, and Eeyore was going to do nothing to stop me. He needed his power back.

As time went on, I was enjoying my new adventure in life and had even taken over a manufacturing company. Yet, I always kept in touch with many of the staff members. They told me that Eeyore wanted his own family working in the business, though they didn't have the skill set, and demanded the staff's respect without giving it back.

As the first year went by, I heard that employees were leaving one by one. I would stop by when I was in town and all I heard was the old complaints. No money, sales have dropped, no support, the gross profit margin needed to be higher, the service department sucked, each branch manager was for themselves, budgets cut, and the list went on. It was a sad outcome. To see a business slipping back into the old habits I had worked so hard to iron out most definitely hurt my soul a bit. Ultimately, the business did go under. However, I think it's necessary to say that I went on to manage another business and we ended up employing many of the old team members and taking over the market. Let the fun begin!

This chapter is included to demonstrate how companies should look at whom they put in charge. Just because the CEO is your son or daughter, does that make them the right candidate for the position? I have worked for family companies for over twenty-five years and I have seen the same thing in a lot of them. Some CEOs from within the family are great of course, but generally, they tend to be more likely to take the business down.

What I hope is that fathers listen to their employees and make sure their son or daughter is ready for this position. Take the time to make sure they understand each department and how it works for the business. Ensure they work with and hire good management and do not be worried if any of these people can do a better job.

You need to look out for the Eeyore CEOs -- they will bring you down and suck you into their world. Do not let this happen. Keep a positive attitude, always stay motivated, and keep your staff far away from Eeyore.

My biggest suggestion, if you happen to work for an Eeyore, is to have a meeting, set some goals with him, and make him go visit customers or accounts with you and your sales personnel. Let him be in front of the customer and hear the problems of the company. You need to help him become a mentor without him knowing it, to take away the workload that weighs him down and to turn him into a Tigger.

This is dedicated to all my friends and colleges that I left behind.

Thanks for that illuminating story, we hope you all moved on to bigger and better things, and that there's a solid lesson for fathers of budding young CEOs. Fathers, you ran your company well probably because you built it from the ground up and know each and every part of it inside and out. Regardless of how smart they are, can your son or daughter manage the same?

CHAPTER 4

The Tweedledee Brothers

The contributor of this story worked for a company in the late 1990s located in New Mexico. If you have ever seen Alice in Wonderland, you'll recognize the brothers Tweedledee and Tweedledum in this story, or perhaps the characters from the movie Dumb and Dumber.

I used to work for a mid-sized corporation that manufactured construction tools. This was a family-owned business running for over seventy-five years that sold to both domestic and international markets. Average sales were around fifty million dollars per year, and they employed two hundred people. They sold their products through distributors that had been with them for, in many cases, the entire time they had been in business, and were loyal distributors.

When I started with the company, the father was the CEO and he hired me to manage the sales and marketing of the corporation. Their father's reputation had been strong with their distributors for over forty years and he had established all the accounts personally. The company had such a reputation that banks would ask them for business and the father was even on a few of the banks' boards. He was a solid leader of a successful company.

A year later, however, the father decided to retire and made his two sons CEO and COO. These boys had grown up in the silver spoon club and had little experience in the real world of business management. On the first day of his new position, the CEO turned up at 9:30 a.m. and the COO finally came rolling in at 11:00 a.m. They immediately called a meeting with the management staff to discuss their new company plan.

They had some big plans and ideas and their new strategy was to grow the sales, lower prices fifteen percent across the board, and increase distribution by setting up more distributors in our market. They advised us to double our staff over the next three months because sales were going to grow, and nothing was going to get in our way. As we discussed this plan, we asked, "How are we going to do this?" After all, the company already had effective and loyal distributions in set territories with contracts that had been in place for nearly seventy-five years. Their strategy was to think of this as a new company with big ideas, which included breaking the current contracts and doubling the distribution houses.

Then the management staff asked, "How are we going to lower the price fifteen percent and maintain margins when we have some products that are in the twenty-five percent to twenty-eight percent gross profit margin range?"

The response from the CEO was, "We will make it up in volume, and this will lower our manufacturing costs."

The last order of business was to hire more staff, and the management staff asked, "How can we do this without knowing what incremental orders we will receive?"

The CEO firmly believed that the orders would come in.

Next, the management staff asked the COO for a business plan, and the brothers said, "You are the managers, figure it out! What are we paying you all for?" Soon enough, the meeting was over, and they adjourned to go play golf for the remainder of the day.

Later that week, the management staff told them that this plan was not ideal. It became clear that it would hurt the company sales and margins. We did some market research, established a business plan, and discussed this with the CFO. The CFO, who had been with the company for over fifteen years, told the brothers that their plan would not work and would destroy the company if adopted. Furthermore, the banks would not look favorably on it and could withdraw our loans, plus their father would go crazy if he found out. The brothers advised the CFO and the rest of the management staff to make it work or they would be replaced with someone that could. They also made it extremely known that no one should contact the father. Ultimately, their last statement was, "He is gone, and this is ours to make a go of it."

As a month or so went by, we had started to hire staff while our sales orders had not increased and our inventory was building each day. We went out looking for new distributors. Being in a close-knit business, our existing distributors found out what we were doing and started to drop our lines. Two months into the "new company directive," we had three fewer distributors than we'd started with. Also, sales had dropped five percent, and gross margin was down almost twenty-five percent. The CEO and COO would come into the office only two to three days a week and only four to six hours a day. The expense accounts they were on would make you sick. The way they spent their money was truly tragic. The company had no direction, morale was sinking fast, and good quality staff members started to jump ship. Not only were we losing employees at the speed of lightning, yet they were started to work for the competition.

When we were about six months into this new program, the CEO called a meeting with his managers and informed us that he was not happy. The CEO felt that the management staff was not doing their job. His biggest concerns were that manufacturing costs were higher, and that we had so many products in inventory. Additionally, he wanted to know why sales were down and why we had added more staff without the sales to support them.

We all quietly made eye contact with those around us as our shock rose.

The CFO reminded the CEO that this was the strategic plan he'd developed, against our recommendation. Thankfully, the CFO explained that management had been following directions.

The CEO turned abruptly to the CFO and said, "Are you that stupid to follow a plan like this? We gave you direction, but your job was to give us the information we needed to make sound decisions to run this company." He continued, "You all should be fired for allowing this to happen!"

Just one day before, the two of them had met their father to discuss the downturn of the company. Both of the sons informed him that it was the management staff that had come up with this new strategic plan. They did not like this plan, they had told him, but as good leaders, they felt they needed to allow their management staff to implement it.

Then, the CEO, in front of all of us, fired the CFO and put the blame on him. The CEO told the management staff to fix this problem. His suggestion was to fire staff, lower inventory, and raise pricing 30% to cover our losses because we were not meeting our projections. We had three months to complete this task, turn this company around and we would have to advise the CEO and COO each week what we were doing to accomplish these goals.

As the CEO and COO were leaving the meeting, the management staff tried to explain that raising the price on our products would not be a positive move because of the competition and the recently lowered pricing. They stood in front of us and said they did not care and directly ordered me to make it work.

Three months later, the company was still losing money and sales were down even further than we had projected. The CEO called a meeting, but this time I was not included. The CEO told the rest of the management staff that the company needed to recruit and hire a more qualified sales and marketing executive to manage the day-to-day sales operations. I was told that they stated that I could not get the job done and I was making them look bad to their father, so I had to go.

That night the CEO fired me.

Two years later, the company had lost six more of the executive management staff, the company sales were down from fifty million to less than twenty million, and the total company employees were reduced from two hundred down to eighty-three. The father decided to sell the company to one of their competitors and did so at pennies on the dollar.

Thanks, contributor, for another cautionary tale about hiring your nearest and dearest to run the company for you, when they don't have the business experience to do the job properly and want to spend their days on the golf course instead. Worse than that, they had the experts they needed, but they were too vain and arrogant to listen to them. That is what brought this company to the ground.

CHAPTER 5

Thank You for the Team, Daddy

This story comes from a guy we'll call Jeff, who worked for a professional sports team back in the year 2000. You're going to see another out-of-control son taking hold of the company reins here with disastrous consequences, but here I'll turn it over to Jeff...

I was the luckiest person in the world, or so I thought. Out of the blue, I received a call from a professional sports team. Somehow, the owner had been handed my resume by a business colleague. The year was 2001, and the team was looking for an executive to manage all their marketing, sponsorship, ticket sales, and run their business development. This was a dream job and there is not a person in the world that would turn this opportunity down.

I had an interview with one of the owners over the phone. Later that day, I was called back and asked if I would fly in for a few days to meet some team members. I couldn't believe my luck, and as I went through the interview process, my heart was beating faster than a train going through Manhattan. Never in my life had I been so nervous and so hungry for a position. After an agonizing wait of a few days, I received a call back from this owner. He wanted me to come back to discuss the position one more time.

So far so good, and as we met, the second time and discussed what he was looking for me to accomplish, I could feel the passion in his voice indicating that I was the candidate for him. This sealed the deal for me; this guy had faith in me. Three weeks later the team offered me the job.

I became the manager of all the marketing, TV, radio, and tickets by which I mean *all* the tickets, including the VIP suites. As a year passed, the position was getting better each day, and I loved what I did. My staff was in place and the owner loved me like a son... Or so I thought. Sixteen months in, I found myself sitting in an executive meeting with the owners. This was when I was informed that Jr. would become the new President and CEO of the team. Jr. is otherwise known as, one of the owner's sons... Shocker. As we all left this meeting, we wondered what was going to be in store in the months ahead.

The first month or so, everything was the same; business as usual. I did my job to the best of my ability. Being the workaholic that I am, seventeen-hour days were normal for me. My staff liked my management style, and we did a great job for the team. I controlled a lot of the large accounts and I was always mingling with high rollers that loved to spend money. Soon enough, I started to see Jr. wanting to get involved with part of the business.

Jr. was a silver spoon boy whose dad had given him everything in life. His father provided for him financially, worked to get him into the best schools, and handed him life on a silver platter. Yet, at this point Jr. was also learning that partying was far more fun than being a young professional. Jr., at twenty-eight, was on the wild side. He was the bachelor of all bachelors; a single guy who "loved" a variety of women. Long story short, we were told numerous times that we needed to "keep a close eye on him" when we were on road trips.

This is a sport in which most teams lose money no matter what, and the owners liked to buy a team because they could. If they ever wanted to sell there would inevitably be a list of clients a mile long looking to buy them out at five times their actual value.

We threw money away every day, and with sports personnel. Once contracts came up, money was a huge deal. This is when the gloves would come off and some brutal nights of negotiation would commence. While negotiations were going on, the office would be open late into the night. I would leave the office sometimes well after dinner time and the CEO's doors would still be closed, though you could hear the screaming as both sides negotiated long and hard.

One night I had taken some of our clients out to dinner and although it was very late, I needed to go back to the office to pick up some tickets I had forgotten to bring to the dinner. As I walked into the office, I saw Jr.'s office lights were on and I could hear some funny noises. That night, I did not stop and listen, but perhaps this was a mistake. Instead, I rushed through the office, grabbed what I needed, and left. The following week I was on a road trip with the team. One of my jobs were to make sure the owner's suite was ready for the game. To go above and beyond, I would invite some out-of-town guests and have them fly in with the owners and the team. This was a huge hit and helped my team increase their sales, each game.

Eventually, I found out that Jr. liked to invite women to travel with him to the out-of-town games and some of them were married. There was onetime Jr. even invited both the husband and the wife along, then once the game started, he and the wife left, and the husband was too involved in the game to notice. I never followed him, but I sure had an idea of what was going on. One night, I went out to dinner with the father and started up a conversation about Jr. I advised him to discuss the issue with his son. The father told me he would take care of this right away.

About a week later, Jr. called me into his office and asked two interesting questions. The first was, "Do you have a problem with me?" and the second was, "Why are you butting into my life?"

I explained that I was just looking out for the team and this was not personal. The next few months were excruciatingly long and hard, and I was walking on a short leash with Jr.

Every day he would try to find something I was doing wrong -- tickets sales were down, there was not enough television revenue, why were we not selling more concessions. You name it; he looked for something.

Then one day it happened. I was invited out to a mayor's dinner with the owners and Bob, in the arena right by our office. It was a gala night filled with press, the team, and anyone who was someone. All I knew was that we needed to keep Jr. in line that night. We talked about Jr. who liked to have fun. After a few drinks, his courage got more intense, meaning that he'd be living on the edge to see what could be accomplished by the night's end. As the party was going on strong and running late into the evening, his father asked me if he could have some game tickets to pass out. It had been made clear that I was the keeper of the tickets and no one was able to give them away, besides me -- not even the owners. This was a necessary check and balance on the freebies. I would never say no, yet my supervision allowed for everyone to feel like someone was tracking who received what.

I informed the father that I would head to the office to grab the tickets, so he asked me to take some press along and give them a tour because we had just remolded some offices and the front entrance, and the team owners were rightly very proud of this. As we walked across the street, I could see that some lights in the building were on, including the executive suite. I signed in with the guard at the front desk and asked if anyone was in the building. He said no, but that he'd just come on duty and the other shift had just left. We took the elevator up to the twenty-third floor and I started the tour.

We started at the main entrance, where we had game magazines in the lobby, and I asked if they would like one. Then we proceeded to the remolded offices. The press was very impressed and asked if they could take a few pictures. I said yes, after all, a free press is always a nice touch. As we came down the hall, I was telling them about the new conference room and how we had designed it with plasma TVs, surround sound, and video conferencing. The owners had offices across the country so if they wanted to have a meeting this meant we could set one up at any time.

As I approached the door to show them the conference room, I did not notice the light coming under the door. I opened the door, with my guests from the press right next to me, only to discover Jr. on top of the conference table with a government official's wife. Of course, they had their cameras out and they started clicking away. Within a few moments, the wife realized they were there, jumped up, grabbed her clothes, ran down the hall and locked herself in the bathroom. Jr. was in shock. I pulled the doors closed and put forth my best effort to calm down the press. As they started to move to the elevators to leave the building, I called the guard and told him to hold them there, no matter what.

That was the longest night of my life. My instincts kicked in as I quickly called the father, some other owners, and our legal department. When they arrived, I explained what happened, and that we needed to take action right away. The government official's wife was still in the bathroom and Jr. was just sitting there with his head on the conference table. I told everyone about the pictures and that we had to take action instantly.

We asked the guard to bring the press upstairs. Within the next few hours, we all discussed a plan and ultimately came up with a contract to purchase the pictures. We paid over one hundred thousand dollars each for the pictures and had them sign a letter stating that this had never happened. Then we settled the government official's wife down and one of the owners escorted her back to the party. Now, it was about what the hell to do with Jr.

Jr. had to give a press conference with the reporters we'd paid off and he gave them an exclusive story. This story was that Jr. was resigning in order to manage a new business they had just purchased. The father who was a thirty-three partner of this team, made a press announcement stating that due to health reasons, he was selling his percentage to the other owners in a five-year deal and would be stepping down from the board of directors.

The family has been in turmoil since that night. The power the father had given to his son had torn into one of the best franchise sports teams and dismantled a family.

Thank you for taking the time, Jeff and the gang.

CHAPTER 6

How You Take a Browbeating and Then Enjoy a Dream

This story was told to us by a client about his dealings with a large tractor manufacturing company and their commercial tractor product. It begins back in November 2009.

Our company was awarded this commercial tractor dealership in Mesa, Arizona. Although we had never sold tractors before, we felt it was an excellent product and that it would be a great addition to our existing equipment offering. During the first six months, we sold double our "quota." We were over the moon.

In April 2010, this company attended a national show in Houston, TX, and part of the show involved us going to dinner with their executive management team. Given our success, I envisioned us (my sales manager and I) being led into the restaurant by a full collegiate marching band with confetti falling on us, culminating with some sort of prestigious medal. Normally, I don't enjoy business dinners, but I was extremely excited about this one because of all the accolades and compliments we were going to be receiving from the company staff and managers.

My sales manager and I arrived at dinner promptly at seven o'clock after figuring that the lack of a marching band and confetti was likely due to some sort of local fire ordinance prohibiting such extravagant productions. We joined the CEO who was already seated. He was a tall man, with big broad shoulders, looking like a Greek god. We had never met him before, but we'd been warned by other dealers, "Don't sit by him, or it will be a long night." Of course, the only two seats open were right beside him. We introduced ourselves and exchanged pleasantries with him and the rest of the management team that was attending the feast. As we were the last ones in the restaurant the CEO had already ordered a crab plate appetizer. We're talking about a massive plate, approximately thirty-six inches in diameter, with a two-foot-high mound of ice cubes on it, sprinkled with dozens of extra-large snow crab claws.

My sales manager and I declined to partake in the crab madness, but the CEO was in the midst of some type of "zone" diet which meant he was continually hungry but could eat as much protein as he wanted and still reach his target. He attacked the mound of snow crab like a pit bull attacking a Yorkie. I had never seen anyone devour so much food in such a short space of time. I tried to sustain some kind of conversation with the CEO and had been thinking this would be an event we'd never forget. However, instead of showering us with compliments, the CEO turned to us and asked why our performance was so dismal. He continued, asking what we were going to do to turn it around, as news of our poor performance had reached the highest levels in the company at their world headquarters in Texas.

As the color drained from my face and I began to feel light-headed, I looked at my sales manager, hoping he knew what the crab-eater was talking about. Seeing the blank look on his face did not make me feel any better. I was now torn between faking a heart attack or saying "F*ck you... take your line and shove it."

Instead, I chose to respond with something somewhere between the two which mainly consisted of stuttering and mumbling.

Finally, my sales manager said, "Your numbers must be incorrect as we are doing quite well."

The CEO's response was, "Prove it! You are one of our worst dealers and I do not know what to do with you."

We made it through the rest of the meal, and I alternated between wanting to throw up and wanting to throw the overpriced crab directly out the window. By the time the CEO had finished his mountain of crab legs and his 64-ounce Porterhouse steak (medium rare), he began to notice I was verging on passing out into my uneaten filet mignon and garlic mashed potatoes. He almost seemed to feel some sympathy for my predicament. I had been told he was heartless and hated all dealers and if he could have sold directly instead, that's what he would have been doing.

Apparently, to make me feel better, he said, "Tell you what, I would like to invite you to play golf at the Cypress Point Country Club with me and some of my guests. This way you might learn how to sell more products, learn from some of my good dealers, and maybe, maybe, you will get some kind of clue how to sell my product."

With that he stood up, we shook hands and he left. I went to my hotel room and lay down in the fetal position until I drifted off into a nightmare-filled, unrestful slumber.

Let's fast forward to October. Having buried this meeting into the dark recesses of my mind, I didn't give the Cypress Point Country Club invite another thought until early in the month, when I received an email inviting me to play golf with the CEO of this tractor company. The invite outlined the dates, protocols, rules, expectations, and requirements for playing at the Cypress Point Country Club. My heart immediately went from a resting fifty-eight beats per minute to a slightly uncomfortable one hundred thirty-five.

I noticed the other fifteen recipients of the email all worked in construction management or for various golf industry companies, so I decided I would get a feel for their golf background, using my CIA-like investigative abilities on Google. Within ten minutes I was able to ascertain that all the other participants were PGA professionals, ranging from a former general manager of Pebble Beach Resorts to a former PGA touring pro who held the world record for the longest drive with an iron (368 yards).

With the big golf event looming eleven days away, I had not yet even removed my clubs from their winter storage spot in my basement. My mind drifted back to how hard I had worked in 2009 to get my handicap down. I immediately went to the membership website to refresh my memory and to see how I'd ended up. I recalled that I had felt pretty happy near the end of that year, as I had reduced it by almost five strokes. But within a millisecond after typing in my password and hitting enter, I saw my handicap come onto the screen and I thought I was having a mild stroke. There it was... plain as day... my handicap after a diligent summer of working hard, concentrating, and playing regularly was 21.

There I was, six months later, having swung nothing more than a baseball bat, while I was eleven days from playing Cypress Point. Luckily my body has an excellent way of dealing with situations such as this—the medical term is called "sweating profusely." I was sitting at my desk in my nice cool office, drenched in sweat, just as one of the girls walked in with some documents to sign. I pretended to have come down with a sudden case of Legionnaires' disease and mumbled something about going home to bed. After she had left, I toweled myself off and planned my strategy. I was able to determine quite quickly that I was doomed and then I spent the next eleven days fantasizing about my plane having mechanical issues. Every excuse in the book crossed my mind, "Maybe I could have my knee explode during a hockey game." This would most definitely save me from the utter humiliation of playing this club with three pros. Unfortunately, my knee was still intact on the dreaded day. Reluctantly, I went to my country club three days before leaving and played nine holes and shot a crisp fifty-five with half a dozen three-foot gimmes.

Before I knew it, I found myself landing in Virginia, picking up my rental vehicle and driving toward the city. Our accommodation was in a cottage located just fourteen minutes from Cypress Point Country Club. The cozy six thousand square foot cottage was fully stocked with beer and cocktails. I expected it to be bustling with activity with all the other guests. However, I arrived at 5:00 p.m. and was apparently the first one to get there. I assumed the others would be along shortly. So, I sat down, made myself comfortable, and waited for my fellow participants -- the golf pros.

I must have dozed off because around 11:30 p.m. I woke up on the couch and still found myself alone. I then started to wonder if I had mistimed my trip. Perhaps I was a day early? Or worse still, a day late. I double-checked my itinerary, but I was there on the right day... just alone. Eventually, I called it a day, crumpled into bed and tossed and turned anxiously.

At some point, I heard voices... loud voices. The golf pros had arrived and were all chatting about their successes on and off the golf course. Of course, I could hear all this perfectly due to my room being directly adjacent to the living room area. Rather than get up, I thought I should try to get as much sleep as I could. In the mental state, I was experiencing, I only drifted off to sleep around 4:00 a.m. and awoke feeling well-rested and refreshed... two hours later.

I showered and dressed and introduced myself to the other participants who were all up, bright, and fresh. As I shook hands with very well-tanned, well dressed, confident golf pros, I thought to myself, "You are absolutely screwed!"

As we drove in the SUV over to the country club, I became more and more nervous as I pictured my drive on the first hole being a two-foot dribbler, or even worse... a complete whiff. I tried not to show my nervousness but even the most unobservant, dim-witted person would probably have seen the pool of sweat accumulating on the floor of the SUV near my feet.

As the shuttle transported us from the parking lot to the driving range, I fantasized about being somewhere else... a happy place, such as Kabul, Afghanistan, or floating alone in the middle of the Pacific Ocean, or camping next to an active volcano. These daydreams calmed me down somewhat. I remained at peace until I saw my fellow participants taking picture-perfect, relaxed swings, and striping their drives a crisp 290 yards to the back of the range.

My first swing resulted in a nice 14-inch divot and an impressive 40-yard sideways slice. Feeling that was as good as it was going to get, I meandered off to the putting range where, in fifteen minutes at a six-foot distance, I was able to sink precisely zero balls. As I was considering vomiting in some nearby bushes, I heard our names being called. We were only eight minutes from our assigned tee time. At this point, I looked down and could see my heart beating under my golf shirt. The only problem was that there didn't appear to be an ambulance nearby, and I was concerned that a heart rate of two hundred fifteen for an extended period for a forty-eight-year-old man might not be sustainable.

We lined up and had our picture taken at the first tee. My smile was similar to the look of somebody having their fingernails pulled out. I normally like to hit first to get it over with but unfortunately one of the pros had beat me to the punch. He confidently lashed the ball down the center of the fairway about 270 yards. As I said, "Nice ball," I was close to physically collapsing which allowed one of the other competitors to get to the tee before me, yet again.

This time his swing was flawless and succeeded at getting the ball just five foot shy of the rough, still in the fairway. He slammed his club in disgust. If I had been in his spot after two shots, I'd have been ecstatic, yet he was calling himself a loser for this "ill-conceived" shot. Again, my lack of attention allowed competitor three to tee his ball up. I didn't see his ball land because he hit it so far that he flew a little mound in the fairway, out about three hundred thirty-five yards. At this point, I started to get tunnel vision as the blood in my body started to leave my extremities.

And then there was one.

I had put on both my rain gloves as my hands were drenched with sweat having the club fly out of my hands would have gotten me banished me from the day's event. I walked to the tee like a condemned man heading to the gallows. I took a couple of feeble practice swings with my three-wood. It felt like I had never swung a club in my life. I tried to calm myself with a couple of deep breaths which only caused my vision to close into a tighter tunnel. My head felt concussed. My heart was beating rapidly, yet irregularly. I was shaking. The golf pros were watching. Some amused bystanders had gathered to observe. I was mumbling "Please God... don't let me embarrass myself... please... I'll do anything... let me hit it eighty-five yards... anything." I tried to convince myself that life comes down to a few key moments... and at that point the only key moment that came to mind was death.

I brought the club back and with every ounce of energy I had left, I swung as hard as I could.

I heard titanium strike urethane, and I opened my eyes, still expecting to be able to read the "Nike" on my ball still sitting on the tee. Instead, I watched one of the most glorious things I have ever seen. My ball was fifty feet off the ground, flying straight and true down the middle of the fairway, silhouetted against a gorgeous blue Virginia morning sky like a Hellfire missile before it hits a 1972 Dodge pickup truck full of Taliban. At about 270 yards out, the ball lost power and altitude and gently dropped into the middle of the fairway, in amongst my fellow players' balls.

I instantly pivoted, strutted back to my golf bag, hiding the happy dance I was ready to burst out in, and I could hear myself saying "How do you like those apples, chumps?"

I don't remember much after that, except I didn't stop smiling the rest of the way around, and when we finished, I looked at my scorecard and it said one hundred and sixteen.

As I was leaving the event, the CEO walked over to me. I was just going to thank him for the time of my life, but he started before a word could get out of my mouth. "I only invite top dealers to this event, and I must have had too many drinks that night to invite you to this once-in-a-lifetime event of mine." Then he asked me if I'd learned anything about his product line, could I sell more products now and did I have what it takes to get the job done. Then before I could say a word, he turned and walked away.

Perhaps I'd never be in that CEO's good books, but I still knew it was one of the best days I'd ever had.

Thanks for the story, ND. For those of you striving to be good enough, sometimes you just need to know that your best was plenty.

CHAPTER 7

Tony Robbins Trained Me to Be A King

This story comes from a guy we'll call Harry, the year was 2015, the business was a trucking company. It was based in Los Angeles California. This was an amazing business as Harry built this up from one water truck to over 400

different trucks in his fleet with different divisions. Each division had a manager that reported to a Vice President of sales and marketing. You had one division that worked with small contractors, one that worked with the private sector, one that works with large projects, and the last one worked with local government projects.

Harry was in his early forties; his father started the trucking business and became a self-made millionaire. Soon enough, daddy retired and promoted the very lucky Harry to CEO. This member of the lucky sperm club was 6' 1" tall, with golden blond hair. He was a man who made sure you knew he was the boss; he had a voice louder than the average African lion. He showed his power as he dressed like he was a banker with his two thousand suites and 750 BMW. Yet, under all of that, he was a gold chain salesperson always selling a story. I will say he would have been a better stage speaker than TR as he had much to offer in some cases. However, he definitely forgot about the big picture, leaving his audience daydreaming for the majority of his talk.

What made this business a struggle was both the employees and the drivers. While some did whatever it would take to make the client happy, there was another 20% that you were praying just showed up for the workday. Then there were the dreaded days that they wouldn't show up at all, throwing off anything the schedule had attempted to keep together. Where the real story begins was not on the employees, yet, once again, on the CEO and how he managed the day-to-day business. This was a huge success don't take me wrong, but I have still never seen a business with such a high turn around.

Let's get back to Harry, he was an outstanding person that could sell anything. He left a stunning first impression with everyone he came across. The words that eloquently flowed from his mouth, left you believing every last word he said.

Then you got to know the real Harry. He would stand in the opening of his office door and yell a name. He did this confidently as if someone would return with a "My king!! What can I do for you?" He would smile and say come to my office.

Harry was a man filled with passion and you could honestly recognize his voice from anywhere. This is where Tony Robbins comes in. Harry was his number one fan. He had trained with him and everything that came out of his mouth was a Tony line. As Harry entered each morning with his piercing, triumphant voice, you would hear, "ARE WE GOING TO STRIVE TODAY?!" loud and clear.

At all meetings, Harry would discuss how to "push harder." He preached similarity. The man would always explain that in sales it was necessary to do the same thing every single time -- talk the same, know what you're saying, keep the client on the phone, and make sure you take the order.

Like I said, the first thirty days of working with Harry, most would leave the meeting feeling like they could take on the world. The issue was that thirty-first day when it was the same lines and then the 300th day with, yet again, the same lines. After day 300, no one wanted to attend the meetings.

Ultimately, employees were coming in and out so quickly that I was reviewing the Vice President of sales and marketing position every three months. Considering that the number one rule in business is to try to keep your employees, this left me dumbfounded. The constant battle of hiring every few months was costing the company loads of money. Overall, the division managers did not care what the vice president would say or try to do. Respect had been thrown out the window as employees and customers knew that they would have absolutely no consistency.

This business was bringing in an average of sixty-five million dollars in sales per year. I had never been to a Tony Robbins training; however, I would regularly remind my employees, "It takes five years to grow a client relationship, and five minutes to lose one."

What I noticed within the first few weeks at this business was that drivers were regularly late. When they were there, they would do an amazing job and the customer would be overflowing with joy. Later, we would receive a call from the customer stating that they were thrilled with the driver's work, but that he failed to show up on time and worked a seven-hour day, rather than an eight-hour day. In my position, I was mainly concerned with the fact that this was hurting our rating and leaving a bad taste in the customers' mouth. Our company had been stained by the drivers' mistakes.

Confusion would strike as Harry would decide to take the driver's word over the customer's. Rather than crediting the customer, he would examine every ounce of the driver's work. Harry was more concerned with keeping his money than with pleasing the customer. The CEO was more inclined to go through the effort of filing paperwork to make the driver appear to have been on time. He would express, "If it was an hour or less, we do not need to do a refund. If it was longer, someone will need to call the customer and ask if we can credit half." By the time our beloved Harry submitted everything and did every ounce of "protocol" it had taken the company 75 days to refund the customer.

Throughout my time working here, the troubles continued. The complaints flooded in. We once received a call from a customer that stated that they had been shorted yet again. Once again, Harry remained stubborn and persistent as he followed each bit of his own protocol. Here we were, yet again, finally refunded the customer on day 75. While this aggravated the rest of the employees, Harry didn't have a single care in the world.

More trauma struck the company one day as I was digging in reports. It came to my attention that someone working in sales had been doing deals on the side to make himself some extra cash. For obvious reasons, this shocked me. I rushed into Harry's office, laid the evidence right before his eyes, and he was unamused. It took over five months, the work of multiple employees working to make up the slack of the lost money, and a ton of anger before Harry finally addressed the problem.

When it came to the hiring staff, there was only more scum under the rug. All the issues stemming from the same root -- Harry's desire to strictly follow his own protocol. The point here is that when a CEO wants to manage everything, the business does not go forward, in fact, it moves at the pace of a snail. Harry would regularly expect someone to be hired within a few days, yet he wouldn't attend the meeting! Without him at the meeting, no one was able to move forward. After all of this commotion, he would yell, "If this team doesn't hire someone by the end of the week, you are all fired!"

When it came time to hire an SEO manager, the same problems arose. There was no getting around Harry's stickler rules of hiring. This led to months upon months of lost income as an SEO manager would rake in money by the load.

What we can all learn from Harry is that no one person can do everything. As a CEO you need to lead yet allow your staff to manage. While I could write an entire novel on Harry, this chapter just scrapes the surface.

For all my friends I made at this company, thank you for the support you gave me and the strides we tried to make.

What can your company take from this story about Harry? How can CEOs better follow protocol without having unrealistic expectations? These are questions you can bring to your team and discuss.

***

Sidenote: Tony Robbins is a registered trade name and anything with his name in this chapter is not about him. Tony Robbins has nothing to do with how this business was managed, what the CEO processes are, or what Tony Robbins' process would be in business. The man is an amazing speaker, coach, trainer, and a huge success. This chapter is about the CEO of this business. I will give my plug to Tony Robbins as I would play a video of Tony during each Monday a.m. sales meeting to get them motivated. Some employees went to a Tony Robbins event to learn about the amazing firewalk. One day I would like to attend this event and even meet him.

About the Author

Michael D Eastwood (Mike) is a seasoned executive with experience in all aspects of corporate business, family business, personal owned business, CEO of a chamber of commerce, and the CEO of a nonprofit. His executive management skills include managing sales, marketing, retail operations, real estate brokerage, day & med spas, engineering, accounting, personal transportation, dealer/distributor networks, and manufacturing operations in a worldwide market. His career has evolved from sales, management, operations, marketing, promotions, advertising, engineering projects, business consulting, and owning his own business. He has held a broad range of positions in sales as a territory manager, sales manager, national accounts manager, director, managing director, executive vice president, chief operations officer, CEO, and chairman of the board. He has held multiple board of director's positions for different companies, nonprofits, and associations.

He has worked with or managed businesses with annual revenues ranging from $400 thousand to $200 million of sales per year. He has been employed with both large and small, public, and private family corporate businesses. Additionally, he has been involved with distribution sales for fifteen years, manufacturing sales for eight years, and business development for nine years. He has also been involved with private capital companies and has spent fourteen years with an international business in the past. His strengths include developing and managing distributor operations, dealer operations, B2B, call centers, catalog sales, hostility service business, real estate brokerage, direct sales/marketing, new product research and developments, working with professional sports teams, the PGA, and retail operations both within the US and in global markets. His successes are attributed to developing strategic plans, which include recruiting, training, P&L management, start-ups, and purchasing a business and opening strategic new retail branch locations/operations. Mike is known as the business turn around, guy!

His passion for business allows him to develop teams with high energy levels that, by working together, have accomplished the missions and visions set out for them. Mike is also a sales manager trainer and business development coach. His tag line is: We grow business... We change lives!

Visit our website at www.bellosol.com or email us at ceostories2020@gmail.com.

Mike Eastwood

www.ingramcontent.com/pod-product-compliance
Lightning Source LLC
Chambersburg PA
CBHW060634210326
41520CB00010B/1600